THE WORKING SCAMMELL SHOW

Barry Brown

FAIRGROUND HERITAGE TRUST

Published by:
Fairground Heritage Trust
Milford
Lifton
Devon
PL16 0AT

ISBN 978-0-9556610-0-6

Printed by RCS plc
Randall Park Way
Retford DN22 7WF

Design and layout by
New Era Publications

This book is dedicated to the memory of the Scammell Showtrac working in its true environment:
the fairground, and as such does not cover their passing into preservation.

FAIRGROUND HERITAGE TRUST

THE SCAMMELL SHOWTRAC

Scammell Motors in 1945 developed and started production of a tractor designed specifically to cater for the needs of the travelling showmen: the Showtrac.

The tractors were based on a standard 20-ton MV chassis but with a wider cab. A Gardner 6 LW diesel engine and Scammell 6-speed gearbox was fitted as standard, although by 1948 there was an option for a 10.35 litre Meadows six-cylinder diesel engine. A 4-ton cast iron ballast block was fitted along with a

Mawdsley dynamo, belt-driven from a gearbox p.t.o. shaft. A water tank was also fitted for cooling the gearbox whilst generating.

Scammells appointed E.G. Brown & Co., a coachbuilding company from Tottenham to build the specially designed bodies. These were of steel construction, with two rear doors, a roller-shutter on each side and a roof hatch. Extras available for the tractors were a 10-ton winch, a pair of easy-fit tracks (EFT) for soft ground and track-grip tyres.

Sidney Harrison Ltd of 26 Westley Road, Bury St. Edmunds was appointed sole agent for the Showtrac. Born in Thetford in 1886, Sidney Odom Harrison followed his father, Thomas, into Burrell's works, but later moved to Fowlers of Leeds. When the age of steam ended he worked as agent for Scammells.

Eighteen were built between 1945 and 1948 and delivered to showmen, although Harrison's records show a nineteenth built , but delivered as a haulage tractor on 23rd February 1948 (chassis number 6576) to Beck & Pollitzer of Southwark Bridge, London, who were Machinery Transport Specialists. This did not have any Showtrac fittings.

Only one Showtrac was actually completed and delivered in 1945. This was ordered directly from Scammells. The customer was Henry Studts of Swansea. The next five were all ordered by Harrison in early 1946 and presumably used stock vehicles sold to showmen and records show that four were delivered to Harrisons with ballast box bodies and one with just a ballast weight.

Most of the Showtracs entered service minus the coachbuilt bodies and were returned later for these to be fitted. After Browns completed the work they were returned to Scammells at Watford for painting and then usually an official works photograph taken of the completed vehicle by Scammell's official photographer, Gregg Cooper & Co. of Watford.

The images on the following pages show the Scammell 4x2 N.C. 20-ton chassis under development for the Showtrac in the works at Watford. They used a wooden mock-up dynamo to work out the power take off and belt drive system for generating. They also show clearly the winch system fitted.

The main section of this book gives a history of each of the Showtracs built, and are listed in order of delivery date taken from the original records of Sidney Harrison.

Left: Original Sidney Harrison Showtrac Advertising Card.

4

Above: Sidney Harrison's demonstrator, which went on to become Pat Collins' KDH141.
Following pages: The official photographs of the first production Showtrac show it in chassis form and fitted with dynamo, ballast block and winch. It is in primer and awaiting road and generating tests.

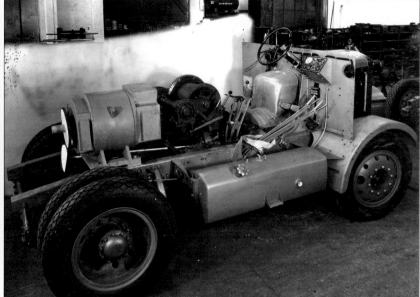

These images show the vehicle with dynamo and winch fitted with all necessary electrical switchgear.

HENRY STUDTS & SONS

Henry Studts & Sons took delivery of *His Majesty* [chassis number 6032] DWN766 on 3rd December 1945. It was probably delivered to his headquarters at Morriston Fairground, Swansea in time for the Ebenezer Street Christmas Fair in Swansea. The nameplate came from an earlier Fowler showman's engine. It was never fitted with a coachbuilt body.

Henry Studts died in 1942 and the business was carried on by his widow, Harriet (nee Dooner) until she passed away in 1948 and then by son Peter, who died in 1951. At this stage the business passed to brothers Edward, Vernon, James and Rowland.

His Majesty was used by Vernon Studt, who travelled an Orton Dodgem track, originally supplied to the firm as a Brooklands Track in 1939. It was converted to a Dodgem in 1946 and travelled until sold to Henry Chipperfield.

The Showtrac remained in use until the 1960s and still survives awaiting preservation.

Above: DWN766, carrying fleet number 3 seen during its working life. *[Studt Family]*

Above: Vernon Studt's DWN766 in its final form with aluminium-clad ballast body, at Pendine on 29th June 1963. *[Philip Bradley-copyright of Surrey History Service]*

Above: The first Showtrac, DWN766, fitted with ballast body, supplied to Henry Studts & Sons.

HENRY ARMSTRONG

On 29th April 1946 HAU964 [chassis number 6109] was delivered new to Henry Armstrong of Nottinghamshire. It was built with a ballast body, easy fit tracks but no winch. A coachbuilt body was never fitted, but it did have chariot sides and a generator was mounted on the back.

Henry Armstrong travelled in the East Midlands and into Yorkshire with the Mont Blanc he inherited after marrying Enoch Farrar's daughter, Dorothy. Later he bought a new Dodgem track and had the Blanc rebuilt as a Toboggan and then a Caterpillar; it was the latter that was lettered on the deep-skirted, high-sided body in the 1950s. It travelled extensively on the run of fairs which came from the original Farrar run, including Nottingham and Hull at the back-end.

In 1966 it passed to E.L. Morley of New Mills, Cheshire, who used it until 1972 with various machines, including a Dodgem track.

It was retired in 1972 and still survives in preservation, but has been fitted with a replica Showtrac style body.

Above: HAU964 possibly before the chariot sides were fitted, alongside E.C. Farrar's Waltzer. Marshall Brothers' Mont Blanc in background at Dewsbury in 1952. *[Rowland Scott]*

Above: Henry Armstrong's Showtrac HAU964 at Aston, Birmingham on 23rd September 1958. *[Philip Bradley—Copyright of Surrey History Service]*

Above: HAU964 in the ownership of E.L. Morley, at Buxton in May 1967. *[Pete Tei]*

Above: Henry Armstrong's Showtrac HAU964 with the loads for his Caterpillar at Aston, Birmingham on 22nd September 1958. *[Rowland Scott]*

ENGLISH'S FUN FAIR

Delivered on 6th May 1946 to Cyril W. English, ACF38 [chassis number 6108] was fitted with a ballast body, but no dynamo nor E.F.T. At sometime a look-alike Brown body was fitted to the Showtrac and lettered in the livery of English's Fun Fair.

Cyril English was originally from Stowmarket and worked in partnership with L. Duell. They travelled two rides. One was a Lakin Noah's Ark, originally new to Whiteleggs and which was sold to Pelhams. It retained in original 'Royal Hunt' extension front and jungle rounding boards for several years until it was rebuilt as a Waltzer. The firm also travelled a Dodgem Track.

Presumably the partnership was dissolved when Mr English and the Scammell moved to the Southampton area in the late 1940s, where the Dodgems were travelling.

The Showtrac was sold into use as a dock-yard shunter in 1952 with Docks Haulage on Southampton docks. It has survived into preservation.

Above: Showtrac ACF38 owned by English's Fun Fair. *[Biddall Brothers Collection]*

Above: Copy of the advertisement placed by Sidney Harrison in the World's Fair when he was acting as sale representative for Scammells with the travelling showmen. As well as supplying Scammell Showtracs and 45-ton chain-drives, he also supplied the Fowler-Sanders generators that were very popular with showmen after the war. This was placed in the *World's Fair* when Sidney Harrison was celebrating 50 years of working with showmen, having been salesman for Burrells of Thetford and later with Fowlers of Leeds, helping design the last four Super Lion showman's engines built by them.

ARNOLD BROTHERS

Arnold Brothers were the customers for EDL111 [chassis number 6074] on 15th May 1946. It was supplied without bodywork or a winch but with E.F.T. It is believed the E.G. Brown bodywork was fitted the following year. Arnold Brothers were based in Southampton, but had a run of fairs which included the Isle of Wight. At the time they travelled a set of Gallopers and a Dodgem track.

Showman Tommy Benson acquired the vehicle over the winter of 1953-54. Bensons are based in Dorking, and travelled some of the finest rides in that part of the country. The Lakin Ben Hur Speedway was new in 1936 and from that time the family always used lorries, never owning a steam engine. Initially a six-wheel Saurer was used with the machine. After the war the firm expanded, acquiring a Dodgem track and in 1949 a magnificent Lakin Swirl. The Scammell joined their fleet of vehicles and worked with the Ark.

The Showtrac is still owned by the family in complete and original condition.

Above: Another view of EDL111 in original livery.

Above: EDL111 hauling the Galloper loads.

Above: Arnold Brothers' Showtrac EDL111 in original livery. *[A.C. Durrant]*

Above: EDL111 on the Isle of Wight ferry.

Above: Thomas Benson's Showtrac EDL111 at Wormwood Scrubs, London in 1967. *[P.M. Photography]*

Above: Thomas Benson's Showtrac EDL111 at Tadworth on 26th June 1980. *[Philip Bradley-Copyright of Surrey History Service]*

JOHN POWELL

John Powell's Showtrac CU4667 [chassis number 6111] was called *Unique,* taking the name from the firm's Foster showman's engine. It was delivered on 21st May 1946 with no bodywork but otherwise fully equipped. It was returned later for the coach-body to be fitted.

John Powell inherited the business from his aunt, Mrs William Murphy, for whom he had worked. When she died her Noah's Ark and Swirl passed to him.

Unique travelled regularly in the north-east of England, working with John Powell's rides, which included the Orton Supreme Speedway, a large Orton Brooklands Track, Swirl and Dodgems. John Powell was one of the consortium of showmen who ran the Hoppings on Newcastle Town Moor and also operated the amusement park at South Shields.

The Showtrac was retired in about 1962 and stored at South Shields. By this time the original windscreen had been replaced. Due to the proximity of the sea the tractor suffered from the salt air.

In 1978 it was smartened up and briefly brought out of retirement in June and taken to Newcastle Town Moor fair, where it ran power for John Powell Jnr's Chair-o-Plane ride, a job it performed on occasions when both returned to the park at South Shields.

When the ride was sold the Showtrac was again retired and apart from a set of modern windscreens and new front wings it is still much in original condition. It is currently in store still owned by the Powell family.

Above: Powell's Showtrac working with the Dodgems on Newcastle Town Moor on 14th June 1960. *[Rowland Scott]*

Above: Powell's Showtrac generating for Powell's Chairs on Newcastle Town Moor in June 1978.

Above: Powell's Showtrac CU4667 *Unique* at Wolsingham in 1950. *[John Gale]*

Above: Powell's Showtrac standing alongside his AEC Matador tractor at Houghton-le-Spring.

Above: Powell's Showtrac lowering the Speedway centre truck off its gantry at Houghton-le-Spring.

HIBBLE & MELLORS LTD.

Hibble and Mellors Ltd of Nottingham took delivery of HTO221 [chassis number 6114] on 30th May 1946. Initially it had no body but was otherwise fully equipped. It returned later for Browns to fit the coachbuilt bodywork.

Messrs. Hibble and Mellor set up in partnership when James Hibble married Theresa Mellors, daughter of Henry Mellors. The firm also included Theresa's brothers. Mornington Mellors travelled a set of Gallopers and later the firm had a Cake Walk.

In the 1930s they expanded, acquiring a Skid in 1936, a set of Dodgems in 1938 and finally an Orton Super Speedway, which could also be used as a Waltzer, in 1939. The rides travelled around the Nottingham area, and the firm was well-known for its distinctively lettered box trucks.

When J.W. Hibble died in 1964 the firm passed to his daughter and son-in-law, Bertie Parkin, but they settled on the south coast and sold the travelling business.

The Showtrac passed to E.L. Morley of New Mills, Cheshire. It worked with his rides until 1973. It is now in preservation.

Above: Hibble & Mellors' Showtrac HTO221 at Nottingham Goose Fair on 29th September 1958. *[Rowland Scott]*

Above: E.L. Morley's Showtrac HTO221 ready to leave the Goose Fair site in October 1966.

Above: Hibble & Mellors' Showtrac HTO221 location unknown. *[P.M. Photography]*

Above: Official works photograph of Showtrac HTO221 at Watford.

Above: Official works photograph of Showtrac HTO221 at Watford.

Above: E.L. Morley's Showtrac HTO221 at Nottingham Goose Fair in 1966.

Above: E.L. Morley's Showtrac HTO221 pulling-off from the Goose Fair in 1966.

JOE ROWLAND & SONS

Joe Rowland & Sons of the West Country took delivery of HRL121 [chassis number 6115] on 3rd June 1946. Originally named *King Carnival* it was fully equipped from new. It was later renamed *City of Bristol*.

J. Rowland & Sons travelled in the West Country, on a run taking in Devon and Cornwall. Their main attractions included a Moonrocket, which was exchanged in 1949 for a Lakin Ben Hur from Reuben Gilham of Southampton. They also had a Dodgem Track.

The tractor remained in mainly original condition apart from the removal of the cab roof overhang and the replacing of the original split windscreen, with a one-piece screen. It was in regular use until 1985 when it was taken off the road but is still owned by the family.

It is worth mentioning that Harrison's records show Hill & Phillips as the original customers for this vehicle.

Above: HRL121 at Saltash in 1967 *[R.M. Collis]*

Above: Joe Rowland's Showtrac HRL121 at Newquay on 23rd July 1958. *[Philip Bradley-Copyright of Surrey History Service]*

Above: HRL121 after alterations to the cab.

Above: Joe Rowland's Showtrac HRL121 *City of Bristol* pulling the Anderton & Rowland organ truck. *[Patrick Chivers]*

FRANK HARNIESS

Frank Harniess worked in partnership with his cousin, Tom Harniess after the war and the pair originally wanted to order four new Showtracs from Sidney Harrison. Unable to meet the request they settled for two Showtracs and two 45-ton chain-drive Scammells.

DDT181 [chassis number 6173] was new on 17th June 1946 with no body. It was returned to Browns later for the coach body to by fitted. It was later fitted with a Mather and Platt dynamo in place of the standard Mawdsley.

Frank Harniess travelled an Orton & Spooner Swirl, which was new to the family in 1949 and the Showtrac worked with this, accompanied by an A.E.C. Matador equipped with a crane to life the heavy gearing.

The Showtrac stayed with the firm until 1969, last being used at Selby Fair in October that year. When Frank retired it was sold and used by Harry Wigfield with his Coronation Speedway. It still survives awaiting restoration.

Above: DDT181 pulling the Swirl trucks onto the Forest for Nottingham Goose Fair.

Above: Official works photograph of Harniess' DDT181 after the fitting of the bodywork.

Above: DDT181 generating for the Skid.

Above: Obviously Nottingham Goose Fair was the best place to catch DDT181 at work. It is seen here arriving on the Forrest on 1st October 1962 with the two trucks for the Orton & Spooner Skid. *[Philip Bradley-Copyright of Surrey History Service]*

Above: Harniess' Showtrac DDT181 with Swirl box truck after pulling down at Nottingham Goose Fair. *[Rowland Scott]*

Above: DDT181 with the Skid trucks at Nottingham Goose Fair. *[Rowland Scott]*

Above: DDT181 at Nottingham Goose Fair. *[Pete Tei]*

Above: DDT181 at Nottingham Goose Fair in October 1966. *[Pete Tei]*

Above: Generating for Harry Wigfield's Orton Ark at Fairford in August 1980.

JOHN FLANAGAN

John Flanagan of Watford ordered Showtrac GUR148 [chassis number 6189] to work with his Lang Wheels Autodrome ride. It was delivered on 26th June 1946 with no bodywork but otherwise fully equipped. It returned later for the bodywork to be fitted.

John Flanagan was the grandson of Mrs Bird, a famous London showlady. He took over her Gallopers in 1928 and continued to travel them for several more years. In 1939 he added a Lang Wheels Autodrome to the business and also had a set of Chairs.

When John Flanagan died the tractor and ride passed to his niece, Alice Webb, and travelled under the name of W.G. Webb. The Showtrac continued to work with the amusements, including the Autodrome, which lost its extension front and had a smaller one featuring Lady Penelope and her famous pink Rolls Royce.

The Showtrac was used until 1974 when it was retired to their Watford yard. Apart from the removal of the roller shutters it remained in mostly original condition. After being damaged in a fire the tractor was sold into preservation in 1989.

Above: Works view of GUR148 after the fitting of the body by Browns.

Above: GUR148 shunting trucks at Watford in August 1969. [*Pete Tei*]

Above: John Flanagan's Showtrac GUR148 before the fitting of the body. [*A.C. Durrant*]

Above: John Flanagan's Showtrac GUR148 before the fitting of the body. Pinner is the suburban setting for this view taken on 27th May 1947, hauling the Autodrome loads. *[Philip Bradley-Copyright of Surrey History Service]*

Above: Official works photograph of Flanagan's Showtrac GUR148.

Above: GUR148 at Ruislip, Middlesex on 5th July 1968 in the ownership of George Webb. *[Philip Bradley-Copyright of Surrey History Service]*

Above: GUR148 when operated by George Webb of Watford, seen at Ruislip in July 1968 with the 'Tunnel of Love' Autodrome in the background. *[P. Seaword]*

ANDERTON & ROWLAND

Anderton & Rowland's Amusements ordered two Showtracs from Sidney Harrison in 1946 after visiting Nottingham Goose Fair to watch the demonstrator at work driving a machine.

DCO212 [chassis number 6190] *Gladiator* was supplied in grey primer but fully equipped on 8th July 1946. It was collected from Watford by George DeVey and Albert Smith and brought to Exmouth. It was intended for use with Anderton & Rowland's Lang Wheels Autodrome but this had still not been delivered so instead worked with the firm's Dodgems, travelled by George DeVey and Gilbert Smith. Its loads were two plate trucks built new for the Dodgems just before the war which were still on solid wheels. It later worked with the Autodrome.

After the 1946 season travelling around the West Country it was returned to Browns, along with *Dragon,* for the bodywork to be fitted. The tractor returned to Scammells again in the winter of 1949 for an overhaul and following this was exhibited at the 1949-50 Olympia Winter Fun Fair by agent, Sidney Harrison.

During the winter of 1968-69 a new body was built by George DeVey and his brother-in-law, Bob Phipps and after an overhaul during the winter of 1970-71 it was back to its original 1946 condition and put back into service, working with George DeVey, one of the co-proprietors of the Anderton & Rowland firm. It is still owned by the family and currently on display at the Dingles Fairground Heritage Centre.

Above: Anderton & Rowland's Showtrac DCO212 *Gladiator.* [*DeVey Collection*]

Above: Official photograph of Anderton & Rowlands' Showtrac DCO212.

Above: Anderton & Rowland's Showtrac DCO212 passing Lanner en route to Falmouth with Dodgems.

Above: Scammell's works photograph showing back and offside of DCO212.

Above: Scammell Showtrac DCO212 generating for the Dodgems, and clearly showing the air filter ordered specially by George DeVey. *[DeVey Collection]*

Above:Anderton & Rowland's Scammell Showtrac DCO212 with loads of George Devey's Dodgems. *[Patrick Chivers]*

Anderton & Rowland

Ordered by Ernie and Nelson DeVey, the second of the Anderton & Rowland Showtracs was DCO265 [chassis number 6209] *Dragon* delivered on 12th July 1946. Again it was new as chassis and cab; the body was not fitted until the end of the 1947 season. This tractor was also exhibited by Harrisons at an Olympia Fun Fair over the winter of 1947-48.

Dragon was used with the Bristol section of the Anderton & Rowland firm and worked for much of its life with the Orton Jungle Ride, later rebuilt as the Speedway. It travelled extensively throughout Somerset, Devon and Cornwall.

During its life *Dragon* carried a couple of interesting colour schemes: during 1959 it was painted white and in 1974 it appeared in a blue and red livery. Both were real departures from the firm's traditional maroon and red, to which *Dragon* was eventually returned. Its windscreen was also altered at some stage.

The tractor was retired in 1981 and is also currently at the Dingles Fairground Heritage Centre.

Above: DCO265 at Babbacombe in 1948

Above: DCO265 at Exmouth on 18th June 1952. *[Philip Bradley-Copyright of Surrey History Service]*

Above: Showtrac DCO265 *Dragon* at Taunton in 1947 before the coach-built body was fitted.

Above: DCO265 shunting trucks into position.

Above: Official Scammell works photograph of DCO265.

Above: Rear/nearside work photograph of DCO265.

Above: Coupling DCO265 to the trucks ready for another journey.

Above: Another view of DCO265 generating for the Speedway.

Above: DCO265 generating for Anderton & Rowland's Super Speedway.

Above: DCO265 carrying the unusual white livery, with the Speedway in 1959.

Above: DCO265 in white livery with Anderton & Rowland's Speedway at Filton in 1959. *[D. Cheverill]*

TOM HARNIESS

The second Harniess Scammell Showtrac DDT180 [chassis number 6188] was delivered on 29th July 1946. It was new fully equipped but returned to Browns later for the bodywork to be fitted.

This tractor was used by Tom Harniess of York Road, Doncaster with his Dodgem track, an Orton ride new in 1937. When Frank Harniess died in 1942 his son, Tom took over the business, working in partnership with his cousin, Frank Harniess. They had the Dodgems, Ark and a new Swirl. Either the Dodgems or Swirl attended Nottingham Goose Fair and Hull Fair on the back-end run, as well as many other fairs on the Harniess run.

The partnership broke up in 1960 and DDT180 stayed with Tom Harniess, working with the Dodgems until he retired to the amusement park at Canvey Island when both Showtrac and Dodgems were sold to Gordon Eddy in 1967.

Eddy named it Melray, after his two sons: Melvyn and Raymond. In Eddy's ownership it was painted in a light blue colour. Eddy travelled the Dodgems along with his Lakin Speedway, originally McConvill's 'Over the Sticks'. They travelled in Yorkshire and the Showtrac was used until the 1969 season when it was scrapped at Selby. This is the only one of the Showtracs not to have survived.

Above: DDT180 with 6-wheel Dodgem box truck at Brierley Common, Barnsley on 16th April 1962.

Above: DDT180 with Gordon Eddy's Dodgems at Hull Fair in October 1967. *[Pete Tei]*

Above: Tom Harniess' Showtrac DDT180.

Above: DDT180 in the ownership of Gordon Eddy at Burton Constable Rally in 1968. *[Peter Seaword]*

PAT COLLINS

Although finished in the livery of Pat Collins, it was actually John Collins of Bloxwich who operated Showtrac KDH141 [chassis number 6210]. It was delivered on 18th September 1946, fully equipped and complete with E.G. Brown bodywork, which on this vehicle was slightly different and heavier. It made its debut at Nottingham Goose Fair that year. This Showtrac was the original Sidney Harrison demonstrator, and exhibited by him at the Olympia Winter Fair over 1946-47, and had to be redecorated in Collins' colours.

A rear-mounted crane was fitted around 1955 and carried the nameplate from *The Leader* after the Foster engine was retired from service.

When the Showtrac was retired in 1966 it was stored at Pat Collins' amusement park at Barry Island, where some restoration was later carried out.

Showman Pepper Biddall acquired the Showtrac in 1989 and a full rebuild was undertaken. It is still owned by the late Pepper's family.

Above: Pat Collins' travel worn Showtrac KDH141 at Nottingham Goose Fair in 1964. The rear crane can be seen behind the body. *[Pete Tei]*

Above: At Olympia in January 1947 exhibited by Sidney Harrison is KDH141 looking splendid in its obviously fresh paintwork. *[Sidney Harrison Ltd]*

Above: Pat Collins' Showtrac KDH141 at Birmingham Onion Fair in September 1949.

Above: Sidney Harrison was in the habit of 'borrowing' Showtracs from various showmen to exhibit at the large Olympia Winter Circus and Fun Fair. He did so between the years 1946 to 1950, obviously in the hope of attracting new customers. Over 1946-47 the guest Showtrac was Pat Collins' KDH141, the one time Demonstrator.

Above: Pat Collins' Showtrac KDH141 at Oldham Wakes on 16th June 1953. *[Rowland Scott]*

Above: Pat Collins KDH141 craning Waltzer platforms at Nottingham Goose Fair on 29th September 1958. *[Rowland Scott]*

Above: Pat Collins KDH141 arriving at Aston with the Waltzer loads on 8th June 1960. *[Rowland Scott]*

Above: Pat Collins KDH141 and LDH253 at Birmingham Onion Fair on 27th September 1961. *[Rowland Scott]*

John Studt

Messrs John Studt of Swansea took delivery of EWN437 [chassis number 6357] on 16th July 1947, with no body or E.F.T. A coachbuilt body was never fitted to this vehicle. Harrison's records show John Studt's widow, Mrs Lydia Studt as the customer. It carried the name *King George V* a name which was originally on John Studt's Fowler engine.

John Studt, born in 1893, was the second son of Henry Studt Snr., and his business began when he took over the 4-abreast Gallopers new for his father. When these came off the road in 1935 they were replaced by a Noah's Ark, known as the Welsh Dragon Speedway. Their amusements were open in Swansea during the Second World War. After John's death in 1945 the firm was taken over by his widow.

In 1962 the Showtrac passed to their son, Edward Tuson Studt, in whose ownership a more modern cab was fitted. For a time it was loaned to his son-in-law, Abie Danter, who used it with his Noah's Ark, but later returned to Studts.

It was retired in 1974 and later passed into preservation.

Above: EWN437 when owned by Edward Tuson Studt, and on loan to his son-in-law, Abie Danter, seen pulling his the Ark loads. *[Terry Agland]*

Above: EWN437 after coming out of service with Studts and having stood for a number of years.

Above: Mrs John Studt's Showtrac at Scammell's Works.

Above: Mrs John Studt's Showtrac prior to delivery, at Scammell's works at Watford.

Above: Edward Tuson Studt's Showtrac EWN437. *[Terry Agland]*

PAT COLLINS

The second of the Pat Collins two Showtracs was LDH253 [chassis number 6358], delivered to Pat Collins' widow, Mrs Clara Collins of Bloxwich, on 18th August 1947. It was fully equipped with its coachbuilt Brown bodywork..

It worked, mostly with the Dodgems, until retired in 1976 to Collins' amusement park at Barry Island.

During its working life it was driven by Collins' manager, Jack Harvey.

After some renovation work was done and after a showing at the 1980 Much Marcle rally the tractor was put on show by the Collins family at the 1981 Nottingham Goose Fair. The Showtrac was eventually sold into preservation.

Above: LDH253 at Nottingham Goose Fair.

Above: LDH253 with Dodgem loads at Nottingham.

Above: Official works photograph of Pat Collins' Showtrac LDH253.

Above: LDH253 at the Goose Fair in 1966, with Hibble & Mellors' Mack pulling off with three loads.

Above: Official works photograph of LDH253.

Above: Pat Collins' Showtracs LDH253 and KDH141 with Foster showman's engine *The Leader* at Birmingham Onion Fair in 1956. *[William Keating]*

Above: Pat Collins' Showtrac LDH253 at Birmingham Onion Fair on 29th September 1949. *[Philip Bradley-Copyright of Surrey History Centre]*

Above: Pat Collins' Showtrac LDH253 with Dodgem Loads at Aston, Birmingham on 8th June 1960. *[Rowland Scott]*

Above: Pat Collins' Showtrac LDH253 at Birmingham Onion Fair on 21st September 1961. *[Rowland Scott]*

ANDERTON & ROWLAND

Anderton & Rowland's third Scammell Showtrac, JYA962 [chassis number 6417], was delivered on 12th September 1947 minus winch but with E.G. Brown bodywork. It was named *John Bull*, a name previously carried by one of the firm's Burrell engines.

John Bull travelled by Gilbert Smith's section of the Anderton & Rowland firm, based in Bristol. It was used mainly with the No. 1 Dodgems. Later it passed to Ernest DeVey, continuing to travel with the Dodgems, accompanied by the 45-ton chain-drive Scammell *Early Beatty* which was also supplied by Sidney Harrison.

It remained original apart from the removal of the cab overhang and the fitting of a new windscreen. It also appears to have carried different liveries, sign-written in various styles. In 1977 it was returned to traditional maroon livery.

It travelled regularly until 1983 when it was retired to the firm's depot on Gloucester Lane, Bristol, having worked its entire life with the No. 1 Dodgems.

It remained in store at Gloucester Lane until moved in December 2001 for proposed restoration, although still owned by Rowland DeVey.

Above: Anderton & Rowland's Showtrac JYA962 at Babbacombe in 1948.

Above: Showtrac JYA962 after alterations to the cab at Shaldon, South Devon. *[P.M. Photography]*

Above: Anderton & Rowland's Showtrac JYA962 *John Bull.*

Above: Anderton & Rowland's Showtrac JYA962 *John Bull* with Dodgem loads at Exmouth on 18th June 1952. *[Philip Bradley-Copyright of Surrey History Centre]*

Above: Anderton & Rowland's Scammell Showtrac No. 6 *John Bull*

Above: Anderton & Rowland's Showtrac JYA962 *John Bull* with the Dodgems. *[Patrick Chivers]*

Above: Anderton & Rowland's Showtrac JYA962 *John Bull* with the Dodgem loads at Penzance. *[Patrick Chivers]*

ANDERTON & ROWLAND

The fourth of the Showtracs built for Anderton & Rowland was JFJ367 [chassis number 6656] and named *The Showman*. Having bought a new Dodgem Track, Sidney Harrison persuaded George DeVey that he should have a new Showtrac to accompany it. When he asked how he was going to pay for it, Harrison made him "an offer he couldn't refuse."

It was delivered to Haven Banks for Exeter Regatta on 21st July 1948 with no bodywork and minus gearbox cooler, winch and E.F.T. A Mather & Platt dynamo was fitted instead of the standard Mawdsley and also a Meadows 10.35 litre six-cylinder diesel engine. The body was fitted at the end of the season.

The Showtrac had a short career with Anderton & Rowland. Despite the generous terms offered by Harrison, he became impatient and it was agreed that the Showtrac would be returned. Two of Deakin's men collected it from Exeter Cattle Market.

Deakins Modern Amusements of South Wales used the vehicle regularly until the early 1970s. It was later fitted with a Gardner engine, requiring the bonnet to be lengthened. It was left in store by Deakins in the early 1970s before being sold into preservation.

Above: JFT367 with George and Ernie DeVey with John Whitelegg at Yeovil during the last season the vehicle worked with Anderton & Rowlands.

Above: Norma and George DeVey in front of *The Showman* in the park at Totnes.

Above: Anderton & Rowland's Showtrac JFJ367 *The Showman* when new with just chassis and cab.

Above: Anderton & Rowland's Showtrac JFJ367 *The Showman* at Babbacombe 1949 *[Harold Cornish]*

Above: Deakin's Showtrac JFJ367 at Stratford Mop in October 1958, still with the Meadows engine fitted and still carrying it's Anderton & Rowland fleet number 7. *[Denis Miller Collection]*

Above: Deakin's Showtrac JFJ367 and Scammell EBR809 with the Dodgem loads, awaiting the pull-on at Stratford Mop in October 1965.

Above: Deakin's Showtrac JFJ367 at Aberdare, Glams., on 23rd June 1963. *[Philip Bradley-Copyright of Surrey History Centre]*

Above: Showtrac JFJ367 in Deakin's ownership at Banbury on 14th October 1969.

THOMAS WHITELEGG

Thomas Whitelegg, the famous West Country showman was the customer for Showtrac JFJ457 [chassis number 6595] named *City of Exeter*. It was delivered on 10th September 1948 minus winch and fitted with a Meadows six-cylinder engine.

It was exhibited at Olympia by Harrison during the winter of 1948-49 in Whitelegg's colours and described as being brand-new; it may well have just been fitted with its E.G. Brown bodywork. It returned to Olympia for the 1950-51 fair, being the last Showtrac built for a fairground customer.

The Showtrac worked mainly with the firm's Lakin Ben Hur Speedway, although they also travelled a Waltzer, Dodgems and later novelties including a set of Hurricane Jets. After Tom Whitelegg's death in 1962 the firm was run by his daughter and son-in-law Rosie and Gerald Shepheard.

In 1964-65 the Showtrac was modernised, with the loss of the cab overhang, a new windscreen and the fitting of box-type front wings with dual headlights. A Gardner 6LW also replaced the Meadows diesel engine in 1967 when it broke its crankshaft. This necessitated lengthening the bonnet.

Its name was changed to City of Plymouth and towards the end of the 1960s the tractor was painted in green and black with the name *'Show-Trac'* on the bonnet sides, quite a departure from the firm's more usual traditional colours to which it was eventually returned. And renamed *City of Plymouth*. It was withdrawn from regular use in the 1970s and survives in preservation.

Above: T. Whitelegg's Showtrac JFJ457 pulling the Ark box truck.

Above: Whitelegg's Showtrac JFJ457 after appearing at Olympia for Sidney Harrison, with Freddie Thomas holding bucket and Arthur and his mother, Mrs Rose Whitelegg on the right. *[Whitelegg Family Collection]*

Above: Whitelegg's JFJ457 shunting trucks in Plymouth in 1967. *[Richard Collis]*

Above: Whitelegg's Showtrac JFH457 *City of Bristol* with new bodywork in 1949. *[Harold Cornish]*

Above: Whitelegg's Showtrac JFH457 *City of Plymouth* pulling the Noah's Ark loads at Penzance. *[Patrick Chivers]*

Above: JFJ457 in Central Park, Plymouth. *[R.M. Collis]*

Above: JFJ457 towing trucks at Haven Banks, Exeter. *[T. Rowland]*

Above: JFJ457 after the alterations to the cab and front wings.

Above: JFJ457 manoeuvring a box truck into position.

Above: Although not strictly a Showtrac, Harrison's records show that a 20-ton ballast tractor [chassis number 6576] was delivered on 23rd February 1948 to Beck & Pollitzer, a specialist haulage company, perhaps a cancelled showman's order. Presumably it had none of the extras available on the Showtrac. Since it never entered showland perhaps it should not have been included in this book, but it is interesting to think there could have been nineteen Showtracs. This image of JXH703 may not be the vehicle supplied by Harrison, but it gives an idea of what it may have looked like. *[Graham Upchurch Collection]*

Above: An impressive line up showing Anderton & Rowland's Showtracs *Dragon and John Bull* with their other Scammell tractors *The Lion* and *Earl Beatty*. In George DeVey's own words the Showtracs were the "best thing to ever come out for the showmen...no other vehicle could match it...wonderful." *[DeVey Collection]*

Acknowledgements

We would like to thank the following people and organisations, without whose help and support this book would not have been possible:

Late Terry Agland; Richard Collis; Harold Cornish; Late Richard Darby; Peter J. Davies;
George & Simon DeVey; Raymond Eddy; R. & D. Jenkins; Late Denis Miller;
Phil Moth; John Powell Jnr.; Stan Savage; Peter Seaword; Roland J. Studt;
Pete Tei; Kay Townsend; Graham Upchurch.

Kevin Scrivens and Stephen Smith of New Era Publications for the design and layout.

Philip Bradley images reproduced by permission of Surrey History Service.

FAIRGROUND HERITAGE TRUST

Without doubt the artefacts assembled by the Fairground Heritage Trust represents the single most important collection of historic fairground items in the country. The collection represents far more than an industrial archaeology from a period when gilded carved work and artistic competence saw the production of some of the most luscious and extravagant shows and roundabouts ever seen. It also represents the heritage of a group of people who are often neglected amongst the itinerant population of Britain. The travelling showmen are an identified social group who are extremely proud of their past but often not in a position to be able to preserve it. In many cases what began life as extravagantly carved, gilded and painted attractions have lost their lustre, and in many cases much more.

Edwin Lawrence's Bioscope Wagon

There is very little left of the days of the Victorian fun fair which offered the working masses of the town of industrial Britain a break from their otherwise dreary and laborious lives. The aim of the Fairground Heritage Trust is to preserve a record of the travelling showmen. In some cases this would be working exhibits, such as the William Wilson's Rodeo Switchback, one of the most famous roundabouts still

surviving in the country from the Victorian period. It would be to restore to its original condition the surviving wagon from Dr Edwin Lawrence's travelling cinematograph show, which lay rotting in a field for over half a century and is now the only surviving example of its kind. It will also see the exhibition of smaller artefacts which represent the lives of dozens more showmen and, using relevant interpretation, help record their family history.

The Rodeo Switchback

Since its inception the Trust has endured a challenging history itself, but a rescue package, put together in 2003 by fairground enthusiast Michael Smith and Richard Sandercock, owner of Dingles Steam Village, has now successfully brought the collection to a permanent home in Devon. A new building was been constructed over the winter of 2005-2006 and the Trust was successful in gaining a Project Planning Grant.

The opening of Dingles Fairground Heritage Centre in 2007 is the result of many years of hard work and unswerving belief in the cause. At present four of the major rides have been assembled at the centre. The oldest of these is the Rodeo Switchback, a legend in itself. Its origins date back to the nineteenth century,

but the fantastic carved figures, two of which are modelled on the cowboy hero Tom Mix, date from the 1920s. It is one of only two surviving Switchbacks in the world.

The Edwards' Chariot Racer Ark is one of the finest surviving examples of its kind. The impressive arched front featuring the Roman Chariot Racing scene was executed by Sid Howell, the finest artist at Orton & Spooner's works at Burton on Trent. The same firm's Dodgems and Swirl occupy the same building and are examples of Fred Fowle, arguably the best fairground decorator of his time.

Anderton & Rowland's Showtracs: Gladiator and Dragon

The Heritage Centre is also home to the Anderton & Rowland Collection, and their two Scammell Showtracs, *Gladiator* and *Dragon*, are amongst the exhibits, along with the Heal family's chain-drive Scammell *Rocket* and their magnificent Orton & Spooner living carriage.

Anyone interested in finding out more about the Fairground Heritage Trust or Dingles Fairground Heritage Centre, should contact the Trust at its registered office: Milford, Lifton, Devon, PL16 0AT, by telephoning the information hotline on 01566 783425, or by visiting the website www.fairground-heritage.org.uk.